D0773565

Ida Skivenes

Eat Your Art Out:

Playful Breakfasts by IdaFrosk

Samlaget
Oslo 2013

Introduction

Breakfast has always been my favorite meal. I particularly love lazy Sunday breakfasts when the table is filled with freshly baked bread, a variety of spreads, pancakes, delicious fruit and a big pot of coffee. But I also appreciate the everyday bowl of hot oatmeal as a good way to kick-start the day.

I grew up on a farm where we always had a well-filled fruit bowl on the coffee table and side salads with dinner. My love of fruits and vegetables, which was acquired at an early age, is something I'm delighted to share with others.

A picture uploaded on Instagram on a whim in the summer of 2012 became the start of an unexpected food art adventure.

My very first food art photo was two slices of toast depicting a bear and a fox. I had seen similar things online and dreamed that someone would serve me such a cute breakfast. When that didn't happen, I took the matter in my own hands and made one myself. The result was so amusing that I decided to post the picture on my newly opened Instagram account. After this I wanted to try out some of my own ideas and discovered, somewhat surprisingly as I can neither draw nor paint, that I had an eye for food art. Somehow I had found my creative medium: food!

So that's how I got a new hobby, which I've mostly been enjoying in the mornings, alongside a fulltime job in statistics by day. I'm not a cook or a professional artist, just an ordinary person who thinks food should be fun. I have no kids yet, so I've made these creations for myself and sometimes for friends and relatives, in addition to my audience on Instagram and elsewhere.

I could never have imagined that my food art would reach the most distant corners of the world. This book is also a way of thanking the many people who have followed my journey, recommending my photos and giving me ideas. Being part of an international environment has meant a lot: I'm not alone in being visually creative with food. Food art has its origins in the Japanese lunch box (bento) tradition, and there are also a few practitioners in the USA today.

Everything you see on these pages was made to be eaten. Even though this is not an "art project" as such, my main sources of inspiration are modern art, cartoons and films. And I do love a good pun! But even everyday events can be inspiring, like what the weather is like or the celebration of a particular holiday. In the beginning I also got inspired by other food artists on the Internet. Playing around with how things appear is not new by any means – in fact, it's part of being human. I think anyone can be creative if they just try, but this book can help you get started. Everything doesn't have to be perfect; and as you can see at the bottom of this page, it doesn't always work out on the first try for me either.

I hope the book will provide some inspiration and entertainment for you, my readers, both when creating your own meals and by allowing you to dream a little.

And for those who don't feel very energetic in the morning: all the meals and recipes can be used for lunch, snacks or an evening meal. Happy eating!

FOOD LOVE FROM IDA

Play with your food!

As a child you were probably told that you shouldn't play with your food. I have heard the same rule myself (but I have obviously not obeyed it as an adult). I think the reason is mostly that parents are afraid of spills or think that the playing will distract from the eating.

Historically, everyone was expected to be happy just to be fed; food was a serious matter with the sole purpose of satisfying hunger. But does it have to be like that today? Isn't it possible to imagine that playing with food is a tribute to the raw materials and all the good things that nature provides for us?

Food can be most inspiring if we allow it to be – with so many different colors, textures and tastes. It's good for both children and adults to activate their senses when eating. If you're allowed to explore shapes and images, it will be fun to eat, not a chore. It may also be easier to try new foods when they are presented in an unexpected way.

Breakfast is at a time when many people have low appetites and could do with something fun to get in a better mood. Imagine getting served a bowl of lion oatmeal or a cat sandwich when you get up. They don't have to take that long to make, and the joy that they spread will definitely make it worthwhile. I've usually made the food in this book before going to work in the morning, so I've tried to stick to simple and quick ideas, even though exceptions occur, particularly on weekends.

Nobody says that you should make food art every day or even every week, but it could be a nice activity every now and then. Having said that, playing with food isn't always appropriate – for instance in a restaurant, or when you're visiting someone. Having good manners applies to both children and adults, and even though you might wish the toast in front of you looked like a moose at sunset, it's not always advisable to start rearranging things. Keep the food art idea in your head and make it when you get home instead.

Using a wide range of fruits and vegetables is important to ensure that you get the whole spectrum of nutrients. It has been said that you should "eat the rainbow". Using this book you can do so literally (see page 40). Here are meals that not only look good and taste delicious; they are also packed with nutrients to provide a healthy start to the day. Some of the food art creations pictured provide too little food for a complete breakfast, so you should make two or add more food on the side to satisfy your own or others' appetites.

One of the questions I'm asked most frequently is: What do you do with the trimmings? It's very important to me to avoid throwing away food. Playing with your food doesn't mean wasting it. Tips as to how you can use leftovers can be found on page 11.

All the food in this book is vegetarian, but of course you are free to use the ingredients you have available. Use your imagination!

Lastly, food art is not just for kids. The best part of making food art as an adult is that you get the opportunity to use your imagination and to reconnect with your inner child. You have complete freedom to play with a myriad of colors, textures and tastes in a creative way. Everyone can find their inner food artist and have fun with food!

GOOD TIPS FOR FOOD ARTISTS

The food art in this book is generally made with common ingredients and simple equipment that most people already have in their kitchen, but here are a couple of tips that can make your work easier and more fun.

When making creative food it's smart to be aware of the color, size and texture of the ingredients used to make an appetizing and different meal. You can use what you have available, but there are some healthy basic ingredients that are often used which you may want to have on hand. These have been summed up in 5 main categories. The basic breakfast foods themselves, like bread or pancakes, are not listed here.

SPREADS
Peanut butter
Greek yogurt
Jam (all colors)
Cream cheese
Sliced cheese

DRIED FRUITS
Dried blueberries
Raisins
Apricots
Prunes
Goji berries

FRUITS AND BERRIES
Lemons
Bananas
Grapes
Blueberries
Kiwis
Oranges
Pomegranates
Physalis
Strawberries

VEGETABLES
Cucumber
Bell peppers (all colors)
Cherry tomatoes
Olives
Sugar peas

NUTS AND SEEDS
Almonds (whole and flakes)
Hazelnuts
Pecan nuts
Walnuts
Coconut (shredded and flakes)
Sunflower seeds
Pumpkin seeds
Flaxseeds

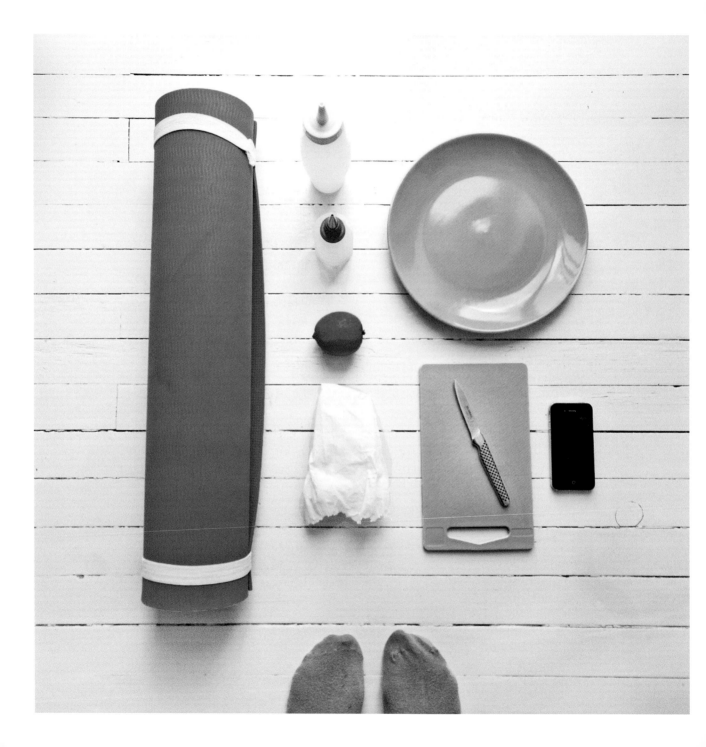

The "tools of the trade" are usually a cutting board, a small knife, a bread knife, scissors and on rare occasion cookie cutters. Optional but practical are squeeze bottles for pancake batter and yoghurt details. An alternative is to use a plastic bag with a small hole cut in one corner, or you can go free hand using a spoon. On the opposite page you can see my personal working kit, which also features a lemon, some paper to clean up as I work, a colorful plate, a rolled up yoga mat to place the finished plate on and of course my trusted cell phone to take the photos.

Doing food art should not mean unnecessary waste of food. I try to use all the food in the creations, but sometimes there are leftovers. You can:

- Eat them while you're concocting your creation (my favorite, particularly in the morning)
- Make fruit salad, or add leftover vegetables to soup
- Put them in your lunch box
- Make croutons or bread crumbs out of leftover bread
- Keep them in an airtight container in the fridge for use the next day

Another good tip is to make the food appealing by using fruits and vegetables in different colors, which will ensure that the food is both nutritious and enticing. A lot of the breakfasts take just a couple of minutes to make if you've planned your purchases and have all the ingredients on hand.

The more "technical" tips are to toast the bread first, as this makes it easier to handle and better tasting. Choose a type of bread that doesn't crumble easily and that has an even shape. Lemon juice can be used on carved bananas, apples or avocados so they won't brown. Greek yoghurt is particularly suitable for food art because it's so thick. It can be colored by stirring in red jam (for pink), blueberry jam (for purple) or cocoa powder (for brown).

INGREDIENTS BY COLOR:

RED
Tomatoes | Red onion | Beets
Strawberries | Raspberries | Jam
Pomegranate | Watermelon
Cherries | Red currants | Red apples
Red plums | Cranberries | Goji berries
Red oranges | Grapefruit
Red cabbage | Radishes
Rhubarb | Red grapes

GREEN
Cucumber | Green bell pepper
Sugar peas | Celery | Salad leaves
Asparagus | Sprouts | Avocado
Pickles | Green olives | Pistachio
butter | Green apples | Green pears
Herbs | Green grapes | Lime
Artichoke | Spring onion
Broccoli | Pesto | Kiwis

BLACK, BLUE & PURPLE:
Black olives | Black currants
Blueberries | Dried blueberries
Black grapes | Blackberries
Figs | Tapenade (olive puree)
Nori (Japanese seaweed)
Wild rice | Licorice

WHITE
Cauliflower | Yogurt
Cottage cheese
Cream cheese
Cheese | Rice
White chocolate
Banana | Coconut

YELLOW & ORANGE
Yellow bell pepper | Carrots | Oranges
Peaches | nectarines | Yellow apples
Yellow plums | Apricots | Yellow pears
Lemon | Ginger | Corn | Sweet potato
Cantaloupe melon | Mango |
Cheddar cheese | Omelet | Pineapple
Honey | Pasta | Honeydew melon
Starfruit | Eggs | Papaya

BROWN
Chocolate spread | Oatmeal
Granola | Peanut butter
Nuts | Raisins | Cinnamon
Bread | Pancakes
Mushrooms | Hummus

RECIPES

Pancakes

For me, pancakes are absolutely the best Sunday breakfast. I like them thick and fluffy — American style. These pancakes taste very good, and are both healthy and filling.

BASIC RECIPE FOR 2 HUNGRY PEOPLE:

2/3 cup cottage cheese
(approx. 150 grams)
2 eggs
1 medium banana, ripe
¼ cup rolled oats
¼ cup finely-ground whole wheat flour
1 tsp baking powder
1/2 tsp salt

VARY THE FLAVOR BY ADDING:
• Lemon peel and poppy seeds
• Blueberries and coconut
• Cinnamon and applesauce (instead of banana)

❶ Mash cottage cheese, eggs and banana together by hand or in a food processor until smooth. A food processor is preferred if you are using a squeeze bottle to make food art designs so the batter won't get stuck in the tip.

❷ Stir the dry ingredients together and add the above. Mix well. The batter should be quite thick. Add some milk if necessary.

❸ Heat a frying pan to medium and fry the pancakes until golden. Serve with fresh berries or fruit.

Hot cereals

A steaming hot bowl of oatmeal is good for your well-being on a cold winter morning. I often use steel cut oats, which are whole grain oats cut into pieces, retaining more of the nutritional value. They might not be available everywhere, so rolled oats or other grains are a good alternative.

Use the same basic recipe for the other types of grain, but read the comments on rinsing and cooking times on opposite page. You can prepare porridge in a variety of other ways as well, the three main methods being: overnight soaking, cooking it on the stovetop or baking it in the oven.

THIS BASIC RECIPE IS ENOUGH FOR 1 PERSON:

1 cup water
a pinch of salt
½ cup steel cut or rolled oats
½ cup milk

❶ Bring the water to a boil. Add the oats.

❷ Now you have two alternatives. If you are making the porridge the night before, you can bring the oats to a boil, put the lid on and set the pot aside overnight at room temperature. In the morning, add the milk and cook for a couple minutes.

❸ If it's already morning you can add the milk together with the oats and cook until tender and creamy, about 30-40 minutes for steel cut or 15 minutes for rolled oats. Add more milk if necessary. Stir in optional add-ins just before the oatmeal is done.

VARY TYPE OF GRAIN:
- Barley (soak overnight, pour off the water, and cook for 30 – 45 minutes)
- Buckwheat (soak for ½ hour, rinse, and cook for about 10 minutes)
- Quinoa (rinse very well and cook for about 20 minutes)

VARY ADD-INS AND FLAVORS:
- Mashed banana and peanut butter
- Coconut and dried apricot
- Apple and cinnamon
- Fresh berries topped with milk

VARY PREPARATION:
Baked: Mix all ingredients in the basic recipe, adding an egg for firmer consistency. Bake in the oven at 200° C (400° F) for about 40 minutes.

Granola

If I want a quick and nutritious breakfast I choose a bowl of homemade granola with ice cold milk and berries. It's very easy to make and can be varied indefinitely according to your own preferences and what you have on hand.

The basic formula for granola is: oats + nuts and seeds + liquid sweetener + oil. To make it even healthier, I choose to substitute a fruit puree or juice for most of the oil. My recipe is not very sweet, so feel free to add more sweetener if you like. If you prefer your granola lumpy, an additional tip is to add an egg white to the mixture before baking. Making granola is simply a matter of experimentation!

HERE IS A BASIC RECIPE THAT I OFTEN USE (8–10 SERVINGS):

3 cups rolled oats
¾ cup chopped nuts and seeds
¼ cup dried fruit
½ cup fruit puree (such as applesauce
*   or mashed banana)*
2 Tbsp oil
¼ cup honey or maple syrup

❶ Preheat the oven to 175 °C (350 °F). Mix the oats, nuts and seeds together in a bowl.

❷ Whisk together fruit puree, oil and honey or maple syrup well together.

❸ Add the liquids to the dry ingredients and spread evenly on a baking sheet covered with baking paper.

❹ Bake for about 20–30 minutes, depending on your oven. Stir the mixture a couple of times for even baking and check often. It's done when it's golden.

❺ Take the mixture out of the oven and stir in the dried fruit. Cool at room temperature and store in an airtight container or jar.

VARY FLAVOR COMBOS:
- Mashed banana, pecan nuts.
- Applesauce, walnuts, raisins, cinnamon.
- Blueberry puree, almonds, coconut, cardamom.
- Strawberry puree, macadamia nuts, flaxseeds, vanilla.
- Peanut butter, sunflower seeds.

Scones à la IdaFrosk

A quick and simple alternative when you're out of bread is to make scones. They're also very delicious! This recipe is for a healthy variety, which makes them figure friendly, being both lower in calories and well suited for making all sorts of figures for food art projects.

BASIC RECIPE (FOR 1-2 PEOPLE):

½ cup finely-ground whole wheat flour
½ cup rolled oats
1 ½ tsp baking powder
½ tsp salt
1 ½ tsp butter
2/3 cup quark or yoghurt
1 tsp honey

❶ Preheat your oven to 175 °C (350 °F). Mix flour, oats, baking powder and salt in a bowl. Work the butter into it with your fingers until it becomes a crumbly dough.

❷ Stir the honey into the quark or yoghurt and add this to the dry ingredients. If using add-ins, for instance chopped apricots and almonds, toss them in now.

❸ Knead the dough carefully until it sticks together, and make whatever shapes you'd like (e.g. a circle, a triangle or some free shape).

❹ Bake for 15–20 minutes until golden. Cool slightly on a rack and serve with cheese or jam. Scones are best when eaten the day they are made.

VARY THE FLAVOR BY ADDING:
• Chopped apricots and almonds.
• Lemon peel and poppy seeds.
• Raspberries and white chocolate .

Nut Butter

A smart spread that contains protein, healthy fats, vitamins and minerals that are good for your body. Nut butter is simply nuts that have been processed in a food processor until the natural oils in them are released. It can be made from all types of nuts, the most common being peanuts, almonds and cashew nuts. The higher the fat content in the nut, the quicker it is to make into nut butter.

THE ONLY THING YOU NEED (FOR 1 SMALL JAR) IS:

5 dl unsalted nuts
½ tsp salt
*Optional add-ins: oil, sweetener, vanilla,
    spices, chocolate.*

VARY FLAVORS:
• Cashew butter with vanilla
• Almond butter with a dash of maple syrup and cinnamon
• Hazelnut butter with chocolate
• Peanut butter with honey
• Pistachio butter with coconut

❶ If you like the nuts best roasted, put them on a baking tray and bake at 175 °C/350 °F for about 10 minutes until they start to smell good and darken slightly. Stir after 5 minutes, and watch closely, as nuts scorch easily.

❷ Pour the nuts into a food processor and process until the spread has the consistency of butter. This takes from 5 to 30 minutes, depending on the type of nuts you've chosen and the power of your food processor. Stop and scrape the nut mixture down from the sides of the bowl from time to time. You can add a bit of oil (rapeseed is good) if you think it is taking too long.

Fruits and vegetables

Little Red Strawberry Riding in the Hood

#strawberries #kiwi #almonds #blueberries #prune #yogurt
TIME: 10 MINUTES

The classic fairytale of Little Red Riding Hood has been reinterpreted using the most delicious of all berries, the strawberry. The shape of the berry is reminiscent of a body; adding some kiwi and yogurt detail brings it all to life. A prune wolf is lurking behind the tree – beware!

❶ Slice a large strawberry in half lengthwise. Cut a circle in one of the halves and fill it with yogurt. Make a face out of pieces of prune and strawberry. Put together the two strawberry halves to make Little Red's body. Use strawberry pieces for the basket and the tiny shoes.

❷ Use the outer, completely green, flesh of a kiwi for arms, legs, leaves and Grandma's house. Slice the remaining kiwi core into long strips that you put together as a tree stem. Place everything together on a plate.

❸ Fill in with details of your choice. Here I've added strawberry mushrooms, scattered blueberries, and a path made out of almond flakes. Eat it before the wolf gets there!

The Black(berry) Sheep

#blackberries #yogurt #kiwi #coconut #granola
TIME: 5 MINUTES

Blackberries, which are both beautiful and nutritious, are extremely versatile. They can become bad weather clouds, curly hair or a sheep's fur. The name of the berry makes it well suited for depicting the black sheep of the family.

❶ Put the blackberries on a plate to form the sheep's body.

❷ Use thick Greek yogurt to make the face and legs, then decorate with small blackberry pieces.

❸ Make a landscape with a kiwi sun and grass from coconut flakes and granola if you like.

You raise me UP!

#pancake #jam #yogurt #almondflakes #grapes #physalis
TIME: 10 MINUTES

In the opening scene of the animated movie "Up", a grumpy old man is taken on an adventurous journey when thousands of balloons lift his house off the ground. Grapes have always reminded me of balloons, and here I got the chance to use a lot of them for that purpose.

❶ Make a miniature pancake shaped like a house, or cut the house out of a slice of bread.

❷ Decorate it with jams of different colors, yogurt and almond flakes.

❸ Cut red and green grapes in half, and do the same with physalis berries. Arrange all these elements on a plate and let the food fly away!

Proud As A Fake Peacock

#pear #grapes #clementine #pomegranate #banana #yogurt #blueberry

TIME: 10 MINUTES

The peacock's plumage is an impressive firework of colors when unfurled. Half a pear and a selection of fruit "feathers" is all you need to recreate this fancy bird as a spectacular fruit plate.

❶ Cut a pear in half lengthwise and place it on a plate.

❷ Add a bit of yogurt and blueberry pieces as eyes, and make the beak and legs out of red grapes.

❸ Put whatever fruit you'd like around it to fill up the space. I've used clementine segments, green grapes, banana slices and pomegranate seeds.

Nature Playing With Nature
(So I Can Play With It Too)

#pear #clementine #cottagecheese #grape #banana #coconut #raisin
TIME: 15 MINUTES

If you use your eyes more actively the next time you head to the fresh produce department, you'll soon discover many strange creatures. Pear penguins are actually more common than you'd think. A few simple steps are all that's needed to make the penguin live happily in an Antarctic environment.

❶ Find a penguin shaped pear. Cut off a piece of the skin with a knife to make the "stomach". Make a small hole near the pointed end that you fill with some cottage cheese and a tiny raisin piece.

❷ Remove the skin from two clementine segments and use them as the penguin's legs.

❸ Make the scenery by adding cottage cheese snow, fish made out of grapes and "snowballs" of banana pieces rolled in coconut.

Oh Lady Bugs, You're Not Bugging Me

#cherrytomatoes #creamcheese #olives #cucumber #sugarpeas #bellpepper #carrot
TIME: 10 MINUTES

If you're looking for an easy and entertaining snack plate, this lady bug landscape is perfect for you. Cherry tomatoes and olives become dainty lady bugs in a bed of sugar pea flowers.

1 Spread cream cheese on the crackers and top with a slice of cucumber.

2 Divide a cherry tomato in half and slice it down the middle, half way through. Slice a black olive crosswise and use one part as the lady bug's head. The rest should be cut into tiny dots that you put on the back of the lady bug tomato. Place the lady bug on the cracker.

3 Make flowers out of cucumber, sugar peas, bell pepper and carrot slices.

Ode To Rainy Mornings

#blackberries #redcurrants #apple
TIME: 5 MINUTES

Add some cheer to rainy days by eating delicious berries. Food art can be a good activity when you're stuck in the house and are about to start climbing the walls. If you don't want to go outside with a real umbrella, make one out of an apple!

❶ Using a sharp knife, cut thin lines through the skin of half an apple in a shape that looks like a leaf. Slip the knife blade carefully under it and slice off the outer layer to make stipes on your umbrella. Drip a couple drops of lemon on the exposed apple parts so they don't brown.

❷ Arrange blackberries at the top of a plate to form a cloud.

❸ Place the apple umbrella underneath and let it rain red currants!

Eat the Rainbow

#strawberries #apricots #nectarines #kiwi #blueberries #grapes #yogurt
TIME: 15 MINUTES

Now you can literally eat the rainbow! I cannot promise gold where it ends — but it certainly tastes lovely. All kinds of fruit can be arranged in the correct sequence according to the well-known acronym Roy G. Biv (red, orange, yellow, green, blue, indigo and violet).

❶ Cut the fruit into small pieces so it's possible to create the rainbow's arc.

❷ Arrange everything on a plate in the right order.

❸ Pour on yogurt clouds and take in the colorful sight!

The Strawberry Santas Stopped By

#strawberry #yogurt #raisin
TIME: 5 MINUTES

Strawberry Santas are a food art classic during the Christmas season, but this is a more nutritious remake. If you're making them for dessert, use fluffy whipped cream with vanilla sugar instead of yogurt – and miniature chocolate chips for the eyes, yum.

❶ Stem the strawberries and cut a small piece off the bottom so they will stand. Then slice each strawberry about 1/3 of the way down from the top.

❷ Pipe in thick Greek yogurt and put the strawberry hats back on. Make a small yogurt tassel on Santa's hat too.

❸ Cut raisins into tiny bits for eyes, and decorate.

Welcome to Banana Airlines!

#banana #raisins #cottagecheese
TIME: 5 MINUTES

It has been pointed out that this plane's technical weaknesses, for instance the missing tail fin, would make it hard for it to be airborne. And here I thought the most critical part would actually be the fact that it's a banana – how wrong could I be.

❶ Slice a banana in two lengthwise. Cut one of these halves in two crosswise for use as "wings".

❷ Make windows out of raisins and arrange them on the banana body.

❸ Decorate with cottage cheese or yogurt clouds. Fly away!

Water You Thinking?

#orange #physalis #starfruit #litchi
TIME: 10 MINUTES

For some reason, strange sea creatures have a lot in common with tropical fruits. Spiked skin, soft parts and strong colors characterize both. Here is a little jellyfish family, with starfish fruits and litchi anemones.

1. Divide an orange in half. Remove the peel with a knife. Cut out the segments in one of the halves and arrange on the plate as shown. Make eyes out of the white parts of the orange peel and top with dried blueberry pieces.

2. Use slices of starfruit for the starfish and litchi halves for anemones.

3. Fold back the husks of physalis for miniature jellyfish; give them tiny blueberry eyes.

Toasts

My Food Self-Portrait

#toast #cheddar #cheese #creamcheese #bellpepper #cucumber #blueberries
TIME: 15 MINUTES

This is my food self-portrait, made with a lot of cheese and bright ideas. I'm out in the cucumber forest wishing you a nice day. Now you can make your own self-portrait: what kind of food are you?

❶ Cut a piece of bread to create the head, neck and torso. Cover it with cream cheese. I've used some plain and a bit mixed with tapenade (olive puree) to create the purple/grey color of the sweater.

❷ Make cheddar hair and pencils for the sweater design; arrange them on the bread. The facial features are made with white cheese, dried blueberry eyes, radish cheeks and mouth.

❸ Decorate with cucumber trees and illuminate the scene with a light bulb made out of more cheese.

Happy Valentine's Day, Love Birds!

#toast #creamcheese #strawberry #orange #kiwi #pomegranate #blueberry
TIME: 15 MINUTES

Celebrate the day of love, February 14th, by making an extra nice breakfast for the one you love. Turtledoves are a familiar symbol of twosome love, here interpreted through toast. The two birds form the two halves of a heart.

❶ Use a heart-shaped cookie cutter or cut out a heart from a piece of bread with a knife. Divide the heart in two so you get two "birds".

❷ Cover with your desired spread; here I've used cream cheese with herbs.

❸ Cut a strawberry in slices lengthwise to use for the wings and the heart above the turtledoves. The beak and legs are fashioned from orange slices, while the branches are strips of kiwi with pomegranate seeds on them.

The Eiffel Tower in Paris, France
(French Toast Version)

#frenchtoast #yogurt #strawberryjam #apple
TIME: 15 MINUTES

The Eiffel Tower was built for the world fair in Paris in 1889. It towers a dizzying 1,063 feet (324 meters) into the air (with its antennae). My version is naturally made with French toast.

❶ Cut a slice of bread into an A shape. Mix together one egg, 2 Tbsp milk and a bit of sweetener or salt. (That will be enough for two slices of bread.) Soak the bread in the egg mixture on both sides. Fry it in a hot frying pan until it's golden.

❷ Put it on a plate and decorate with yogurt in the characteristic grid pattern. Carve a piece of red apple into a flag to fly from the top of the tower.

❸ Decorate with hearts and a mouth made of strawberry jam.

The Opera House in Sydney, Australia
(Macadamia and Apple Toast Version)

#toast #macadamiabutter #apple #grapes #coconutflakes #papaya
TIME: 10 MINUTES

The Sydney Opera House was designed by Danish architect Jørn Utzon. Since its opening in 1973, this has been an important arena for concerts and performances of many kinds. The choice of toppings was inspired by the fact that Granny Smith apples originated in Australia and macadamia nuts are a big Australian export commodity. Not to mention the tastiness and look of it all!

❶ Cover a slice of bread with macadamia butter or other light spread. Cut a green apple (preferably Granny Smith) into thin slices that you place on the toast.

❷ Make sailboats out of red grapes and coconut flakes.

❸ Let the sunshine pour in by making a sun out of half a macadamia nut and papaya pieces (or whatever you have on hand).

The City Hall in Oslo, Norway
(Brown Cheese Version)

#toast #browncheese #cheese #almonds #cucumber #blueberry #apricot
TIME: 15 MINUTES

Oslo's city hall, which was opened in 1950, is colloquially called "the brown cheese" – so it was pretty obvious what topping would be ideal here. This cheese is a typical Norwegian specialty that foreigners often meet with wariness. Perhaps it'll be easier to persuade others to try it if you present it in the shape of the city hall?

❶ Cut a slice of bread into the shape of the city hall by cutting off a square at the top. Cover it with a matching piece of brown cheese.

❷ Decorate with small pieces of white cheese for windows and the clock face.

❸ Place it between the blueberry seafront, almond flake cobble stones, cucumber trees and an apricot sun.

Big Ben in London, UK
(Cucumber Sandwich Version)

#toast #creamcheese #cheddar #cucumber #olive #bellpepper
Time: 15 minutes

On this plate English afternoon tea traditions meet a well-known London icon, the clock tower on the Palace of Westminster: Big Ben. The clock was installed in 1959. The typically British cucumber sandwich has inspired the choice of ingredients.

❶ Cover a long slice of bread with cream cheese and make vertical stripes in the spread with a knife. Decorate with strips of yellow cheddar cheese.

❷ Make the clock dial out of cucumber and black olive pieces.

❸ The two-story bus and tower guard are made out of red bell pepper with cream cheese and olives.

How Now, Brown Cow?

#bread #browncheese #cheese #blueberry #grapes #apricot #cherrytomato
#sugarpeas
TIME: 10 MINUTES

As I grew up on a farm with dairy cows, I'm quite familiar with these curious creatures – even though I didn't often take part in their care. The combination of brown and white cheese is surprisingly tasty. I recommend trying it!

❶ Cut out a piece on the top of a long slice of bread so that two pointy ears are formed.

❷ Cover with a slice of brown cheese and cut off pieces to use as ears and horns. Use a knife or scissors on the sliced white cheese to make a round piece for the mule and small bits for spots, forehead hair and eyes.

❸ Divide a red grape in two for nostrils, and make the small tongue and ear pieces out of another red grape. Use blueberries for eyes and make flowers out of sugar peas and cherry tomatoes. An apricot sun is a cheerful addition on top.

Don't Go Nuts!

#scones #nutella #yogurt #almondflakes #blueberry #strawberry #almonds #apricot
TIME: 15 MINUTES (AFTER BAKING)

Figure shaped scones can be the starting point for many food art adventures. This squirrel has been decorated with things made from nuts, which are any squirrel's favorite food. The tail had been made "bushy" by adding almond flakes.

❶ Make scones (see page 21) in the shape of a squirrel. Split each scone in two.

❷ Apply a thick layer of Nutella or other nutty chocolate spread. Add some yogurt on the tummy, around the mouth, for the eye and inside the ear. Cut a tiny piece of dried blueberry or raisin and place it in the eye.

❸ Push almond flakes onto the tail so it becomes bushy.

❹ Place the squirrel on a plate and arrange whole almonds at the bottom, half a strawberry in its paws and an apricot sun above.

A Distant Cousin of Bambi
(On Thin Ice Here)

#scones #peanutbutter #nutella #yogurt #sunflowerseeds #banana #clementine #blueberry #prune

TIME: 15 MINUTES (AFTER BAKING)

Bambi the deer is almost the definition of cute as it struggles to keep on its feet in the Disney film. A sweet combination of spreads seems apt for this creation: Nutella and peanut butter. Pretty and delicious!

❶ Bake scones (see page 21) shaped like a deer. Alternatively you can cut a slice of bread or pancake to shape. Spread it with peanut butter and chocolate spread. Add the white details in yogurt with a spoon or bottle.

❷ Top with two small banana slices, using orange and dried blueberry for the eyes. A small prune can be used as a nose. Sunflower seeds work well for the characteristic spots that a young fawn has on its back.

❸ Remove the skin from two clementine segments and place them next to each other to create a butterfly. Make the antennae out of blueberries.

The Polar Bread Bear

#bread #creamcheese #olive #bellpepper

TIME: 5 MINUTES

The idea behind this polar bear came from a particular kind of bread that we have in Norway, called "polarbrød" – polar bread. The similarity in words inspired this creation. You can use any kind of round bread, or make your own.

❶ Cover the bread with a layer of cream cheese.

❷ Slice a black olive crosswise into rings. Use the closed end as a nose and two whole rings as eyes. Cut the remaining olive rings into two for the ears and mouth.

❸ Cut three strips of red bell pepper for a scarf, or bow tie, if you like. The paws are simply rounded pieces of bread.

Put On Your Hat and Mittens

#scones #strawberryjam #yogurt #grapefruit #blueberry
TIME: 10 MINUTES

The winters in Norway can be long, gray and cold. That's when it's extra nice to warm up with freshly baked scones or rolls and a cup of steaming hot tea. Luckily the citrus fruits are the very best at this time of year and a useful vitamin C supplement.

❶ Make scones shaped like mittens or cut these shapes from bread or pancakes.

❷ Add a layer of jam in your favorite flavor, and use a piping bottle or plastic bag with Greek yogurt to decorate the mittens.

❸ Half a slice of grapefruit or orange can be added as a hat, topped with a blueberry tassel.

Feed the Panda (and Yourself)

#bread #creamcheese #prune #figspread #blueberry #celery #cucumber
TIME: 10 MINUTES

Pandas eat an incredible amount of bamboo: from 9 to 14 kilos in a single day! Maybe this can be an inspiration for you to eat more vegetables too? This panda has been fed celery and cucumber as a substitute for the bamboo.

❶ Spread cream cheese on a slice of bread. Flatten two prunes of about equal size and attach them as ears.

❷ Use fig spread (which comes in sheets that can be cut) or two more prunes for the eye patches and the mouth. Pipe on a bit of cream cheese for the eyes and add a dried blueberry in the middle.

❸ Use a cutter to make cucumber stars, and let celery stalks serve as bamboo shoots.

The Princess on the Sugar Pea

#bread #cheese #brie #celery #salad #bellpepper #sugarpea

TIME: 15 MINUTES

Who hasn't had a restless night, when it seems absolutely impossible to sleep? It can be convenient to have something to blame it on, and if you're proclaimed a princess in the morning, then it's not so bad after all. Sugar peas are a nice stand in for the usual green pea.

❶ Slice cheese and brie into strips that you put on the bread for mattresses. Let a bit of bread be left bare at the top where the princess goes.

❷ Cut a circle of white cheese for her face, make her mouth out of red bell pepper, her hair and crown out of yellow bell pepper.

❸ Add a salad leaf as bedcovers and use celery for the bedposts. Split a sugar pea down the middle and place it underneath the bed.

Holy Breakfast, Batman!

#bread #blueberryjam #almondflakes #apricot
TIME: 5 MINUTES

Batman is one of the classical superheroes, an ordinary man in an extraordinary costume who is fighting for justice in a world of injustice. His iconic silhouette is easily recreated using a slice of toast. If your Batman toast leaves you still hungry, you could always make a Robin to go with it.

❶ Cut off a small piece at the top of a slice of toast so that you get Batman's pointed "ears".

❷ Cover the toast with blueberry jam or chocolate spread. Leave an oval area near the bottom uncovered. Add two equally sized almond flakes for the eyes and cut an almond piece for the mouth.

❸ If you like, make a bat symbol by squeezing an apricot flat and cutting it with a knife or scissor.

Fly Me to the Moon!

#scones #creamcheese #cherrytomato #bellpepper #cucumber #grapefruit
#babybel
TIME: 5 MINUTES (AFTER BAKING)

Let your food take you on a journey into outer space with a tasty rocket that guides you towards cheese moons, a grapefruit sun and black coffee holes!

❶ Make dough for scones, shape into a triangle and attach two small wings on the side. Bake, let rest a minute, and carefully slice in two. You can also cut a slice of bread into the right shape if you prefer.

❷ Apply cream cheese, then decorate with strips of yellow bell pepper, cherry tomato and a triangular cucumber slice at the top.

❸ Using a star-shaped cookie cutter, cut out cucumber slices to make a starry sky. Add a yellow Babybel cheese as a moon, slice a grapefruit in two for the sun and pour up a black coffee hole.

Cat Paw Softness:
To All the Cat Lovers Out There

#bread #peanutbutter #banana #almondflakes #raisin #pumpkinseed #grapes #pomegranate

TIME: 5 MINUTES

Most people consider themselves either a cat or a dog person, based on which animal they prefer. I'm a cat person myself, so I made this cat toast as a tribute to everything that says meow.

❶ Cut out a piece, leaving two ears at the top of a slice of bread. Cover with peanut butter.

❷ Place two slices of banana on the lower half, and push three almond flakes carefully into each side. Squeeze two raisins flat, place them above the banana slices and put a pumpkin seed on each for a fierce cat's eye.

❸ Slice red grapes into triangles for the ears, nose and tongue. Arrange halved grapes with four pomegranate seeds for each of the surrounding cat paws.

Moose at Sunset

#bread #peanutbutter #blueberry #apple #orange #raisin #sunflowerseeds
TIME: 10 MINUTES

"Moose at Sunset" is a common national romantic cliché in Norway. By the end of the 1970s such paintings were to be found in a great many Norwegian homes. My interpretation was created for a TV show called "Around Norway"; the moose is made with just one slice of bread and apple antlers.

❶ You can make the moose out of a single slice of bread. Cut the head of the moose out of the area beneath the stomach. Cut the remaining bits on the side in two so that you get four legs. Move the head to its proper place. Cover everything with peanut butter.

❷ Cut a dried blueberry in two and add for eyes. Use sunflower seeds as nostrils and a raisin for the tail. Cut a slice off a small apple, divide it in half crosswise and make the edges jagged. Use these pieces for the antlers.

❸ Cut off the outer skin of a kiwi before shaping it into a tree. Decorate with blueberries for the proper forest feeling. The sunset is made out of orange and apple parts.

Crazy Like A British Scone Fox

#scones #yogurt #strawberryjam #blueberries #prune #kiwi #plum
TIME: 5 MINUTES (AFTER BAKING)

Foxes are cunning creatures: they are smart and a bit unpredictable. This is just what the expression "crazy like a fox" refers to. Here's a kinder version of this red robber of the forest, made out of scones with yogurt and jam.

❶ Make dough for scones. Shape dough into a fox's head and a small tail. Bake in the oven, let cool and cut carefully in half. You can also cut the shape from a slice of bread or a pancake.

❷ Spread it with an even layer of strawberry jam. Decorate with yogurt on the face, inside the ears and at the tip of the tail. Add two dried blueberries or raisins as eyes, and a small prune as a cute nose.

❸ Cut a tree out of kiwi, use plums as the stem and add some blueberries for the taste and a forest look.

Charlie Brown Cheese

#bread #browncheese #cheese #figspread

TIME: 15 MINUTES

Charlie Brown is the rather insecure protagonist of the comic strip Peanuts. He often runs into bad luck, so you can cheer him up by creating this brown cheese sandwich tribute. Similar shapes can also be used to create other characters.

❶ You will need about 1 ½ slices of bread to make Charlie Brown. Use a knife to shape the torso, saving the strips that you cut off from the side as arms and legs. The half slice becomes the rounded head and neck.

❷ Cut out pieces of brown and white cheese to cover everything.

❸ Make the pattern on the sweater using fig spread or flattened prunes. The same goes for the facial features. Cut a small tuft of hair from a piece of white cheese. Assemble on a plate and chomp away.

The Art Toast Project consists of edible remakes of major works by famous artists, using a piece of toast as the canvas. The idea is based on a literal interpretation of "food art" combined with the desire to make art more accessible.

Frida Kahlo: *Self Portrait*

#toast #cheese #olive #pear #kiwi #strawberry #orange #yogurt
TIME: 45 MINUTES

The Mexican artist Frida Kahlo (1907–1954) is particularly well known for her colorful self-portraits with many elements from nature. This painting from 1940 is called simply "Self Portrait". My version is made out of cheese, with strawberry and olive facial details; the artist is wearing a pear sweater and is surrounded by a kiwi forest.

Vincent van Gogh: *Sunflowers (4th version)*

#toast #passionfruitcurd #yogurt #fig #apricot #raisins
TIME: 30 MINUTES

Vincent van Gogh (1853–1890) was a Dutch painter and pioneer of the Post-Impressionist movement. He is known for his seductive landscape paintings with strong and sweeping colors, and his series of sunflower pictures. This art toast is inspired by the painting "Sunflowers (4th version)", which he painted while staying in the French town of Arles. My sunflowers are made out of apricots and raisins, placed in a fig vase. The background is yogurt and passion fruit curd.

Piet Mondrian:
Composition in Red, Blue and Yellow

#toast #cheese #bellpepper #blueberry
TIME: 10 MINUTES

Piet Mondrian (1872–1944) was a Dutch painter known for his characteristic grid pictures using the primary colors red, blue and yellow. The artwork recreated here is a part of the series "Composition in Red, Blue and Yellow".

Mark Rothko: *Yellow, Red, on Orange*

#toast #marmalade #cherryjam #passionfruitcurd
TIME: 5 MINUTES

Mark Rothko (1903–1970) was an American painter who is often classified as an abstract expressionist, even though he rejected this label himself. He typically painted large single-colored squares that transition into each other. I attempted to recreate this effect by using jams of different colors in my version of the artwork "Yellow, Red, on Orange" from 1954.

Andy Warhol: *Banana Cover*

#toast #banana
TIME: 1 MINUTE

The American artist Andy Warhol (1928–1987) was particularly known for his so-called "pop art". He played with elements from advertising and popular culture, and produced portraits of both Marilyn Monroe and the Norwegian Queen Sonja. The work that is referenced here is the album cover Warhol made for the band The Velvet Underground & Nico. It shows a banana stencil which later has become a familiar symbol of pop art and has been much recreated in street art.

Pablo Picasso:
Marie-Thérèse Leaning on One Elbow

#toast #cheese #bellpepper #tomato #blueberry #creamcheese
TIME: 30 MINUTES

Pablo Picasso (1881–1973) was a Spanish painter who became widely influential. He is widely known as one of the founders of Cubism. He was a prolific artist, producing about 20,000 artworks during his lifetime. The piece recreated here is titled "Marie-Thérèse Leaning on One Elbow". It is one of Picasso's many surrealistic portraits of women, made even more unreal in this cheese and bell pepper version.

Renè Magritte: *Son of Man*

#toast #cheese #figspread #apple #creamcheese
TIME: 20 MINUTES

René Magritte (1898–1967) was a Belgian surrealist known for his witty and thought-provoking paintings. This self-portrait, entitled "Son of Man", shows a man with a green apple hanging in front of his face. It's about the natural human curiosity to find out what is hidden – but here it's only cheese!

Edvard Munch: *Scream*

#toast #creamcheese #celery #cheese #bellpepper #olive
TIME: 30 MINUTES

Edvard Munch (1863–1944), a Norwegian painter and print artist, was an early representative of expressionism and had 60 productive years as an artist. "The Scream (of nature)" is one of his most famous paintings, and there have been many recreations of this motif. But none with cream cheese, celery and bell pepper – until now!

Edvard Munch: *Madonna*

#toast #creamcheese #cheese #cucumber #bellpepper #olive #sesameseeds
TIME: 30 MINUTES

This is the painting "Madonna" or "The Loving Woman" by the Norwegian painter Edvard Munch (1863–1944). The woman in this picture has been interpreted in many different ways: as Mary, mother of Jesus, as a femme fatale and as a vampire. My interpretation is quite different: seductive cheese, cucumber and olives.

Edvard Munch: *Girls On A Jetty*

#toast #browncheese #cheese #bellpepper #olive #cucumber
TIME: 40 MINUTES

Edvard Munch (1863–1944) painted "Girls On a Jetty" in 1901. The scene is from Åsgårdstrand in Eastern Norway, where Munch had purchased a house a couple of years earlier. The mystical girls wearing cheese dresses and bell pepper hats are standing on a pier of Norwegian brown cheese. The cheese and olive mansion house towers in the background.

Henri Matisse: *Icarus*

#toast #yogurt #poppyseeds #apricots #figspread #cranberry
TIME: 30 MINUTES

Henri Matisse (1869–1954) was a French painter especially known for his use of color and his brush strokes. This painting from 1944 is titled "Icarus". Poppy seeds are used in an endeavor to recreate his iconic use of the color blue.

Salvador Dalí: *The Persistence of Memory*

#toast #pesto #cheese #olive #bellpepper #figspread
TIME: 30 MINUTES (EXCLUDING BAKING)

The Spanish artist Salvador Dalí (1904–1989) was a famous surrealistic painter, and his "melting clocks" have become iconic. To illustrate the melting I made two versions of this art toast photo, one before and one after baking. This is the version before baking. The painting is called "The Persistence of Memory".

Claude Monet: *Water Lilies*

#toast #pistachiobutter #apple #kiwi
TIME: 20 MINUTES

Claude Monet (1840–1926) was a French impressionist painter who is particularly known for his striking landscape paintings and series of water lily pictures. This artwork is simply called "Water Lilies". The characteristic green color of pistachio butter was well suited as a background for the apple and kiwi water lilies.

Oatmeal and yogurt

Pigheaded

#raspberryyogurt #raspberries #blueberries

TIME: 1 MINUTE

Some ideas are so simple that they take you by surprise, and this raspberry pig was one of them. Freshen up your yogurt in no time with raspberry nostrils and blueberry eyes.

❶ Pour raspberry yogurt into a bowl.

❷ Add two raspberries as the pig's ears, and two with the openings facing up as nostrils.

❸ Blueberries make the pig's eyes; if you like you can use a dab of natural yogurt underneath for the white of the eye. The mouth is a piece of blueberry cut to shape.

Taj Mahal in Agra, India
(Rice Pudding Version)

#ricepudding #mangosauce #cinnamon
TIME: 15 MINUTES

The mausoleum Taj Mahal is one of the seven wonders of the world. It was built in the late 1600s in memory of Shah Jahan's third wife, Mumtaz Mahal. I chose to recreate this monument using rice pudding with mango sauce and cinnamon, as this is a common combination in India.

❶ Use thick rice pudding. Place it on a plate and shape two towers and a dome using a knife or spoon.

❷ Add mango sauce or mango slices as doors and windows. Use the sauce to make a little pool in front, fencing it off with pieces of cinnamon stick.

❸ Decorate with cinnamon.

Hello Morning Tired Panda!

#oatmeal #blueberryjam #banana #blueberry #prune
TIME: 5 MINUTES

Early morning is probably not the time when you're feeling your freshest, and many of you (and me) probably have quite an empty expression before the day is properly on its way. Having telltale heavy, dark bags under your eyes is not uncommon, and that was the inspiration for this panda porridge.

❶ Pour thick oatmeal into a wide bowl or on a plate. Shape round ears at the top with a spoon.

❷ Make two small pits a bit above the middle and fill these with blueberry jam to create the characteristic black panda eye spots. Top with banana slices with a dried blueberry or raisin in the middle.

❸ Add a prune for the nose, and use thin lines of jam for the mouth. Apply some jam on the ears, and eat away.

A Dog's Breakfast

#cottagecheese #weetabix #grapes #hazelnuts #prune #sunflowerseeds #banana
TIME: 10 MINUTES

This breakfast dog is probably a mongrel, perhaps poodle meets unknown mutt. Feel free to create your very own new breed according to your own wishes.

❶ Fill a plate or bowl with cottage cheese. Add two Weetabix on the sides as ears.

❷ Use hazelnuts for eyes, a prune for the nose and sunflower seeds for the mouth.

❸ Split a green grape in two and place it on top as a bow. Make a dog bone out of banana.

Attempted to Make a Fierce Breakfast, Ended Up With a Friendly Lion Instead

#oatmeal #apple #raisin
TIME: 5 MINUTES

Roar! Every time I try to make something scary it seems to end up cute, but perhaps it's just as well not to get too frightened at the breakfast table. Use this wild idea the next time you're making oatmeal with apple, raisins and cinnamon.

❶ Make oatmeal and pour it into a bowl. Stir in some cinnamon if you like.

❷ Cut a red apple in thin slices and place along the edge all the way around. Reserve one apple piece for the triangular nose.

❸ Use raisins for the eyes and mouth.

Cottage Sheep

#cottagecheese #grapes #kiwi #clementine

TIME: 5 MINUTES

A simple and fun way to present cottage cheese! Sheep already look like they were made out of the stuff, with their lumpy and soft fur. Add a few grape pieces to make the illusion complete.

❶ Make two mounds of cottage cheese in different sizes on a plate. Cut grapes in half for the sheep's heads. Strips of grape can also be used for the legs, ears and eyes.

❷ Use two slices of kiwi as grass.

❸ Add clementine segments as mountains.

In Hope That the Leaves and Birds Will Return Again

#yogurt #kiwi #grape #pomegranate #oatmeal
TIME: 5 MINUTES

Celebrate Spring or rejoice in the thought of it by making this yogurt tree with kiwi leaves. It can be a fresh breath of air on a gray day. Make it into a complete meal by using a thicker layer of yogurt and add more oatmeal as the ground below.

❶ Shape yogurt into the tree stem and branches on a plate.

❷ Cut a kiwi into small pieces and use them as leaves. Add pomegranate seeds as flowers. Sprinkle oatmeal as the ground.

❸ Slice a grape in half lengthwise and make a tiny wing and beak out of kiwi. Use a tiny drop of yogurt for the eye.

The Special Variety of Papaya Kiwi Carrots Found Only in My Kitchen

#papaya #kiwi #yogurt #granola
TIME: 5 MINUTES

It's always fun to trick someone and this is your chance. They might be favorably surprised, as having carrots in your yogurt is probably not so pleasant. If you don't have papaya, another yellow or orange fruit, such as mango or oranges, also works well.

❶ Cut triangular pieces of papaya. Make a small hole in the top of each one.

❷ Peel a kiwi and slice off the outer, completely green, parts. Cut triangles that you make jagged at the top. Adjust the size at the bottom to fit in the holes in the papaya carrots.

❸ Layer the rest of the fruit (cut into small pieces) alternately with the granola and yogurt, then poke the papaya carrots into the top and add the kiwi stems.

Polar Both Inside and Out

#oatmeal #coconut #banana #prune #blueberry

TIME: 5 MINUTES

A warming bowl of polar bear oatmeal with coconut sprinkles. So simple and perfect for the cold, dark mornings.

1 Prepare oatmeal. Top it with shredded coconut if you like; it's really tasty and looks nice.

2 Cut a banana into slices, and add two as ears.

3 Use dried blueberries or raisins for the eyes and a small prune for the nose. Serve hot!

Pancakes

So Jawsome! (That's Sharkasm For You!)

#pancake #blueberryyogurt #blueberries #figspread #almondflakes #banana
TIME: 10 MINUTES

This breakfast was inspired by the 1975 movie *Jaws*. I haven't seen the entire film myself because of a somewhat strained (though unjustifiably so) relationship with sharks. But this breakfast makes sharks seem a lot less scary.

1. Make a roundish pancake and cover it with blueberry yogurt.

2. Add two dried blueberries or raisins for eyes. Cut a piece of fig spread or other suitable ingredient for the mouth; decorate with sharp almond flakes for a fierce expression.

3. Place fresh blueberries on the plate for "water" and cut out a little man from a piece of banana to try out his luck swimming at the top.

Happy Groundhog Day!

#pancake #yogurt #almondflakes #blueberries #kiwi #grapes #orange #physalis
TIME: 10 MINUTES

The USA and Canada have many strange celebrations, and one of them is Groundhog Day. On February 2nd events are held in some communities to see if spring is near. According to folklore, this is determined by whether groundhogs can see their shadows when they come out of their burrows.

❶ Make six pancake pieces (or trim a couple of large ones). Use one for the dirt pile (add a bit of cocoa powder to the batter to make it darker), one for the face (with two small ears), two as paws and two miniature ones for the nose area.

❷ Decorate with yogurt, almond flakes and blueberry eyes.

❸ Cut out and arrange kiwi stems and grape tulips. Make a sun out of physalis and orange segments.

Somewhere Under the Rainbow Lives the Candy Cane Narwhal

#pancake #yogurt #jam #blueberry #grape #kiwi #orange #pomegranate
TIME: 15 MINUTES

Narwhals are strange creatures, , with a tusk in an odd twisted shape that can become up to 2.7 meters long, in an odd twisted shape. In the Middle Ages narwhal tusks were sold for many times their weight in gold because it was believed that they were the healing horns of unicorns.

❶ Make a pancake in the shape of a narwhal. The fin can be made separately and placed on top.

❷ Decorate with jam and yogurt, with a dried blueberry for the eye.

❸ Cut up fruit in different colors and create a rainbow.

Goldilocks & Her Gang

#pancake #mango #yogurt #blueberry #pomegranate
TIME: 10 MINUTES

Goldilocks and the three bears is a strange fairytale, with Goldilocks breaking into the bears' house. No wonder they got upset! The pancake version is easy to make and goes well with honey (which bears love, of course).

❶ Make four pancakes: one completely round for the face of Goldilocks and then three differently sized bear faces.

❷ Cut a suitable mango slice for Goldilock's hair, decorate with pomegranate seeds and place it on the pancake face.

❸ Use yogurt and dried blueberries to complete the design. Taste to see which pancake is JUST right.

I Dedicate This To All Mothers, Past And Present

#pancake #yogurt #strawberryjam #blueberry #grapes
TIME: 20 MINUTES

Russian Matryoshka dolls are symbols of fertility and motherhood. The wooden dolls of decreasing size nestled one inside the other seem to go on forever. Here the dolls are recreated using pancakes, with the same design repeated four times.

❶ Make four different sized pancakes in a bowling pin shape.

❷ Apply the strawberry jam coats first, before filling in with yogurt for the face and apron.

❸ Cut pieces of blueberry for hair and eyes and use red grapes for mouths and apron flowers. Repeat four times (or as many as you have the patience for).

The Great White Whale

#pancake #yogurt #blueberry #grapes

TIME: 5 MINUTES

In Herman Melville's novel *Moby Dick*, the main character Ishmael is on an eternal hunt for "the great white whale", but he never finds it. This pancake is decorated with white Greek yogurt. The dish goes well with a bit of honey on top. Delicious!

❶ Make a whale shaped pancake. Cover it evenly with yogurt.

❷ Use a suitably sized blueberry for the whale's eye and more for his spout and the surrounding water.

❸ The mouth and seagulls are cut out from red grapes.

Owl Always Love You

#pancakes #almondflakes #blueberry #kiwi #physalis
TIME: 10 MINUTES

Owls have an aura of awe and mystery about them. They are considered the wise creatures of the forest and the symbol of bookish knowledge. This owl mother and her owlet have almond flake wings. They are resting peacefully on a kiwi branch.

1 Make six pancakes: two bodies in different sizes, and two pairs of half-moons as wings to go with them.

2 Cover the pancakes in yogurt. Use almond flakes to make the wings, ears, beaks and claws. Blueberries make excellent eyes.

3 Cut strips of kiwi and arrange them as a branch. Make a deep cross in a few physalis and place them on the plate.

The Gloomy Giraffe Wondering About What the Norwegian Winter Season Will Bring

#pancake #yogurt #blueberry #grapes #goji #peanutbutter

TIME: 5 MINUTES

Norwegian winters are probably an unknown concept for most giraffes, but you can wonder what they would think if they ever experienced one. The idea for this giraffe popped up when I was eating a rolled up pancake and realized it might make a nice long spotted neck.

❶ Spread a (relatively thin) filling of your choice on two pancakes. (I used peanut butter here.) Cut off some thin strips at the side of one of the pancakes to be used for horns and a tree. Roll up the rest of the pancake for the neck and place it on a plate.

❷ Fold the other pancake together into a triangle by first tucking in the sides; then make the top with the two pointy ears.

❸ Put the horns in place and top with green grapes. Pour two drops of yogurt and add some dried blueberries for the eyes and nostrils. Make a little tree on the side if you like. Mine is decorated with dried goji berries, but you can use whatever you have on hand.

The Little Prince Eats His Breakfast

#pancake #blueberryyogurt #sunflowerseeds #kiwi #banana #pomegranate
#physalis #grape
TIME: 20 MINUTES

The Little Prince by Antoine de Saint-Exupéry is one of the best-selling books in the world. The story is about a young prince who lives on an asteroid before one day embarking on an exciting journey into the universe.

❶ Make a round pancake with two small volcanoes and cover with blueberry yogurt. Add flowers made of sunflower seeds and place on a plate.

❷ Make the prince's clothes of kiwi, using pomegranate seeds for his bow tie and his belt. Fashion small shoes out of red grapes. The head and arms are made of banana, while the hair is from a physalis. Black sesame seeds can be used for the eyes and mouth.

❸ Divide several physalis fruits in two and place around the asteroid as planets before you pipe on some yogurt details. Join the prince on his travels!

Up, Up and Away (With a Stowaway)

#grapefruit #pancake #blueberry #almonds #cottagecheese
TIME: 5 MINUTES

Travel up into the sky with a hot air balloon that's rich in vitamin C. Stowaways may sneak in, beware! Here, the ears of a funny bunny stick up over the edge of the basket.

❶ Make a square pancake or use a slice of bread. Cover with your desired spread and decorate with sunflower seeds and red grapes. Add blueberries to hold up the balloon basket.

❷ Divide a grapefruit or orange in two for the balloon itself.

❸ Add cottage cheese or yogurt clouds on the sides and sneak in a stowaway using two almonds.

Have a Fin-tastic Day, Little Mermaid

#pancake #yogurt #strawberry #kiwi #blueberry #orange #physalis

TIME: 20 MINUTES

The red hair of the little mermaid Ariel was always fascinating to me when I was a child. The color of ripe strawberries is quite similar. Let yourself be inspired to serve an underwater pancake landscape. And if you're a daredevil, take the plate with you in the bathtub.

❶ Make a pancake shaped like a mermaid. You can also cut out this shape from bread.

❷ Cover it with yogurt. Add kiwi slices, a physalis bikini and strawberry hair. The eyes are made out of dried blueberries or raisins. The mouth is a tiny piece of strawberry.

❸ Make wavy seaweed out of kiwi, starfish and lobster Sebastian out of strawberries and Flounder the fish out of orange and blueberries.

Snow White and the Seven Berry Dwarfs

#pancakes #jam #yogurt #raspberries #blueberry #prunes
TIME: 15 MINUTES

After the poisonous apple scare, Snow White changed her fruit of choice to another delectable red edible: raspberries. The seven dwarfs followed suit with brand new raspberry hats. Make this and dance a silly dance because it's so tasty!

❶ Make a pancake shaped like Snow White. It's easier if you make the arms separately. Make seven small round pancakes too.

❷ Apply Greek yogurt for Snow White's face, arms and other details first. Fill in with blackberry or blueberry jam for her dress. Make her hair out of prune pieces, and use dried blueberries to create her eyes and eyebrows. Top with raspberry details (mouth, hair bow, stripes on her dress and a berry in her hand).

❸ Arrange the seven miniature pancakes around Snow White, top with raspberry halves as hats and draw yogurt details on their faces.

© Det Norske Samlaget
www.samlaget.no
Publisher: Det Norske Samlaget
International distribution: Kontur Forlag
Photo and text: Ida Skivenes
Cover photo: Ida Skivenes
Design: Johanne Hjorthol
This book is typeset in Ideal Sans
Printing and binding:
Scangrapic, Aalborg, Denmark
Printed in Poland
ISBN 978-82-930-5317-0